February 25, 2000

To Merrill,

Best Wishes

Duncan Dobie

IF YOU'VE EVER SEEN A RHINOCEROS CHARGE . . .

IF YOU'VE EVER SEEN A RHINOCEROS CHARGE ...

BY DUNCAN DOBIE
ILLUSTRATED BY TOM SEXTON

Killer Whale Productions

A Division of:
Bucksnort Publishing, Ltd.
Marietta, Georgia
1994

Published by

Killer Whale Productions

A Division of:
Bucksnort Publishing, Ltd.
P.O. Box 670794
Marietta, Georgia 30066

Manufactured in the United States of America
Library of Congress Catalog Card Number: 93-74574
ISBN 0-939801-02-7

Second Printing

The reproduction of the art for this book was
accomplished using filmless, computer-driven
cameras at DIGITAL PHOTO SYSTEMS in
Atlanta, Georgia. This new technology is far less
damaging to the environment than traditional film,
color separations, and chemical processing.

Production of this book was done at the studios of
Digital Photo Systems.
(404) 815-9590

This book was printed on recycled paper. A portion of the
proceeds from the sale of each book is being donated to the
conservation and protection of endangered animals throughout
the world.

*To Bill Drath, a gifted artist, a wonderful human being,
and a man who knew unicorns. You touched a lot of lives
including mine, and the world is richer because of your love
and friendship....*

IF YOU'VE EVER SEEN A RHINOCEROS CHARGE
ESPECIALLY ONE THAT'S GRAY AND LARGE —

IF YOU'VE EVER HEARD THE LULLABY
OF A HUMPBACK WHALE IN MID-JULY —

HE'LL TOUCH YOUR HEART AND DO MUCH MORE...

WILL HE GO LIKE THE DINOSAUR?

IF YOU'VE EVER SEEN A GRIZZLY BEAR
EMERGING FROM ITS WINTER LAIR —
A SOW WITH CUBS IS A SPLENDID SIGHT...
MUST THEY LOSE THE NOBLE FIGHT?

IF YOU'VE EVER SEEN AN EAGLE SOAR

HIGH ABOVE A LONELY SHORE —

WITH SIX-FOOT WINGS AND PIERCING CRY...

HE'S CALLING OUT... SHOULD WE REPLY?

IF YOU'VE EVER SEEN A WHOOPING CRANE

DANCING IN A FIELD OF GRAIN ——

WITH SCARLET CROWN AND BLACK-TIPPED WINGS...
WILL EXTINCTION END THE SONG HE SINGS?

IF YOU'VE EVER SEEN A JAGUAR SWIM
OR STALK ITS PREY FROM A HIDDEN LIMB —
THIS GALLANT CAT DESERVES TO LIVE...
IS A LITTLE SPACE TOO MUCH TO GIVE?

IF YOU'VE EVER HEARD THE MOURNFUL TUNE
OF A TIMBER WOLF BENEATH THE MOON —

SHE SENDS A MESSAGE LOUD AND CLEAR . . .
IT'S GETTING LATE . . . WHY WON'T WE HEAR?.

IF YOU'VE EVER SEEN A SEA COW PLAY
IN THE SPARKLING WATERS OF A COASTAL BAY—

WITH THE SCARS OF MAN ACROSS HER FRAME . . .
SHE HOLDS NO MALICE . . . BUT WHO'S TO BLAME?

IF YOU'VE EVER SEEN WILD HORSES RUN
ACROSS THE DESERT IN THE MORNING SUN —

WITH THUNDERING HOOVES, THEY'RE FREE AS THE WIND...
BUT THE DESERT GROWS SMALL...
WILL THEY SOON BE FENCED-IN ?.

IF YOU'VE EVER HEARD A TIGER ROAR
IN A STEAMY JUNGLE AT HALF-PAST FOUR—
HE ANNOUNCES HIS PRESENCE TO FRIEND AND FOE...
BUT HIS CALL FADES QUICKLY...
WILL THERE BE AN ECHO?

IF YOU'VE EVER SEEN A HARMLESS BLACK SNAKE
ABOUT TO SUCCUMB TO A MAN WITH A RAKE —
SUCH USELESS SLAUGHTER IS HARD TO DEFEND...
WHY CAN'T WE SEE?   THE SNAKE IS OUR FRIEND!

IF YOU'VE EVER STOOD SILENT AND LOOKED EYE-TO-EYE
AT A SHAGGY OLD BUFFALO 'NEATH A MONTANA SKY —
YOU'LL SEE HOPE FOR THE FUTURE, REGRET FOR THE PAST,
HE WAS ONCE ON THE BRINK... WILL THIS LESSON HOLD FAST?

IF YOU'VE EVER SEEN A WHITE-TAILED FAWN
FRISKING IN THE MIST AT DAWN —

WITH WHITE-SPOTTED COAT AND LONG-LEGGED GAIT,
HE'S LIVING PROOF THAT IT'S STILL NOT TOO LATE!

THE LOGGERHEAD TURTLE SHEDS A BIG TEAR
FOR CALIFORNIA CONDORS AND TINY KEY DEER,
FOR ORANGUTANS AND CHIMPANZEES,
FOR AFRICAN ELEPHANTS AND MANATEES,

FOR GIANT PANDAS AND IVORY BILLS,

FOR ALEUTIAN GEESE AND GUADALUPE SEALS,

FOR FLORIDA PANTHERS, THE LIST GROWS LONG —

WHAT WILL IT BE LIKE WHEN THEY ARE GONE?

WHAT WILL IT BE LIKE? DOES IT SEEM FAIR?.
IF THE OCEANS DIE, AND THE FORESTS TURN BARE...
IF THE RIVERS ARE POISONED, AND SO IS THE AIR...
WILL ANY LIVING CREATURE STILL BE HERE TO CARE?

ATOMIC WASTE AND OIL SPILLS,
GLOBAL WARMING AND VAST LANDFILLS,
CONCRETE JUNGLES AND ACID RAIN...
HOW MUCH HAVE WE REALLY GAINED?

TIME IS SHORT... THERE CAN BE LITTLE DOUBT —
MOTHER EARTH'S CHILDREN ARE ALL CRYING OUT!
BUT SHE'S ALWAYS BEEN WILLING TO GIVE US A CHANCE
TO TURN THINGS AROUND...
TO LET THE WHOOPING CRANE DANCE!

IF WE STOP THE POLLUTION, IF WE LEARN TO CONSERVE...
IF WE GIVE ALL OF GOD'S CREATURES THE SPACE THEY DESERVE...
WE CAN SAVE THE PLANET... WE CAN CHANGE THIS SAD TREND...
AND JUST MAYBE MANKIND... CAN BE SAVED IN THE END!

Afterword

Did you know that:

⌒ Acid rain has poisoned millions of fish, killed other wildlife, destroyed forests, and contaminated the soil.

⌒ Pollution from oil spills has contaminated oceans and coastal bays, killed thousands of fish and animals, and fouled many coastlines.

⌒ An estimated 40-50 million acres of the world's rain forests are being destroyed each year. Already, more than 1/10 of the Amazon rain forest has been cut down.

⌒ Toxic waste has polluted streams, rivers, and oceans; killed millions of fish and animals; and contaminated the soil and the ocean.

⌒ Contrary to media propaganda and widespread misinformation by some animal rights groups, ethical hunters have done much to help threatened and endangered wildlife and to save habitat over the past 80 years. Hunters have provided billions of dollars through taxes and private donations to help fund hundreds of crucial wildlife projects throughout the world for both game and non-game species alike. For many years, organizations such as The National Wild Turkey Federation, Ducks Unlimited, Safari Club International, and the Boone and Crockett Club have purchased land, preserved wetland habitat, donated money, and provided manpower to help hundreds of wildlife projects.

The current status of some of the world's threatened, endangered or extinct animal species is as follows:

Lost forever:

⌒ **Passenger Pigeon**   Once numbering in the millions in the eastern U.S., passenger pigeons were exterminated by market hunters during the late 1800s. The last passenger pigeon died in captivity in September 1914.
Status: Extinct.

⌒ **Ivory-Billed Woodpecker**   Once fairly common in isolated swamps in the southeastern U.S., the cutting down of old-growth forests and loss of nesting sites around the turn of the century contributed in part to the decline of this largest member of the woodpecker family. Recent sightings have been reported in remote parts of Louisiana and Cuba, but it is doubtful any survive.
Status: Thought to be extinct.

Threatened or endangered:

⌒ **Bengal Tiger**   In the early 1970s, less than 2,000 tigers survived in the wild. Thanks to conservation and protection, their numbers have increased to just under 4,000. However, continued loss of habitat and human encroachment make the tiger's future questionable.
Status: Endangered.

⌒ **Mountain Gorilla**   Less than 450 in the wild. Poaching for body parts has greatly reduced wild gorilla numbers.
Status: Seriously Endangered.

⌒ **Florida Manatee**   One-fourth of all manatee deaths are caused by boats. It is estimated that nearly 80 percent of all Florida manatees have been injured by boat propellers. Many have suffered crushed skulls, others have had flippers amputated. Today, less than 2,000 manatees survive in coastal waters, but measures are being taken to protect them from boats.
Status: Endangered.

⌒ **Florida Panther**   Less than 50 Florida panthers are believed to exist in the Everglades of southern Florida. Because of serious habitat loss, it is doubtful they will survive in the wild.
Status: Seriously endangered.

⌒ **Florida Key Deer**   The smallest sub-species of native North American white-tailed deer, the population of the diminutive Key Deer once dwindled to less than 50 animals. Due to serious conservation efforts, numbers have now grown to an estimated 300 animals. However, increased mortality from collisions with automobiles continues to be the Key Deer's greatest threat.
Status: Endangered.

⌒ **Whooping Crane**   Never numerous in the U.S., loss of nesting habitat in the Great Plains region saw whooping crane numbers reach an all-time low of 14 birds in 1938. Captive breeding and egg-hatching programs and protection have increased numbers to approximately 230 birds.
Status: Endangered.

⌒ **California Condor**   Once thought to be extinct, this largest of all land birds in North America was rediscovered in 1947. Thanks to protection and captive breeding programs, numbers have now reached just under 50 birds. However, habitat loss and the condor's extreme sensitivity to human pressure make it's survival in the wild very questionable.
Status: Seriously endangered.

⌒ **Grizzly Bear**   Eliminated from much of its former range over portions of the U.S., less than 1,000 grizzly bears now survive in the lower 48 states. Because of habitat loss and confrontations with humans, these numbers will probably decrease in the future. However, an estimated 50,000 grizzly bears survive in portions of Canada and Alaska, and populations are stable.
Status: Protected in some areas.

⌒ **Polar Bear**   At one time, as a result of indiscriminate killing, numbers declined to about 5,000 animals worldwide in the polar regions of the Northern Hemisphere. Today, numbers are estimated to be about 40,000 animals, thanks to protection and conservation efforts.
Status: Protected.

⌒ **Rhinoceros**   Prized for their horns, heavy poaching in recent years and loss of habitat have caused a dramatic decline in all five sub-species of rhinos that still survive.
Status: African White Rhino – Protected in some areas.
       African Black Rhino – Seriously endangered.
       All three species of Asian rhinos are endangered.

Timber Wolf Extinct over much of its former range in the lower 48 states, the wolf has been relentlessly persecuted for centuries. Efforts to reintroduce wolves in some areas of the U.S. like Yellowstone Park have met with serious resistance by ranchers. In all likelihood, the wolf will never be able to live compatibly in these areas. However, timber wolf populations in portions of Canada and Alaska are strong, and should remain strong for years to come.
Status: Red wolf – Endangered.
Timber wolf – Plentiful but protected in some areas.

Jaguar Extinct over much of its former range in North, Central, and South America. Eliminated from the southwestern U.S. by 1900. Today, it is estimated that fewer than 1,000 jaguars survive in Mexico, and less than 200 survive in Argentina.
Status: Endangered.

Guadalupe Fur Seal Once thought to be extinct, a colony of 14 seals was discovered off the California coast in the early 1950s. Through conservation and protection, Guadalupe seals today number about 1,500.
Status: Protected.

Koala Numbers have been greatly reduced due primarily to habitat destruction. Koalas are absent over much of their former range across Australia.
Status: Protected.

Chimpanzee Numbers have been greatly reduced over much of Africa due to poaching and habitat loss.
Status: Endangered in some areas.

Whales and porpoises:

Humpback Whale Slaughtered relentlessly for centuries by whalers. Only a few thousand remained in 1966 when they were protected. Since then, numbers have increased slightly.
Status: Protected.

Blue Whale Protected in 1966. In mid-1980s, North Pacific populations were believed to be fewer than 1,700 animals; North Atlantic populations numbered only a few hundred.
Status: Endangered.

Right Whale Protected in 1935. Thought to be less than 1,000 in North Atlantic waters.
Status: Endangered.

Porpoises Some species of porpoises are declining because of fishing nets and pollution.
Status: Most species still plentiful, some threatened.

Success stories:

American Bison Slaughtered for their hides by market hunters during the late 1800s, only a few hundred buffalo survived around the turn of the century. Today, captive herds across North America number well over 100,000 animals.
Status: Protected in some areas.

White-tailed Deer By the late 1800s, hungry pioneers and hide hunters had virtually wiped out the whitetail population in many eastern states. In 1900, total whitetail numbers across North America were estimated to be less than 500,000 animals. Today, thanks to highly successful restocking programs and modern game management techniques by state wildlife agencies, numbers are now estimated to be around 20 million!
Status: Thriving! (Except for the Florida Key Deer).

Bald Eagle Pesticides and indiscriminate killing greatly reduced the numbers of all birds of prey. Since the banning of DDT in 1972, bald eagles have made a strong comeback over much of their native range.
Status: Protected.

American Alligator Hunted for their hides for decades, alligators were thought to be on the brink of extinction by the late 1950s. They were protected in 1967. Today, alligators are once again numerous over most of their former range.
Status: Protected.

How you can help:

Support national and international wildlife and conservation organizations in their efforts to save plants, animals, and habitat.

Learn as much as you can about nature and about wildlife management techniques.

Lobby both local and national political representatives and presidents of big companies to curb air and water pollution and to protect wildlife habitat.

Help others to learn about endangered wildlife, cleaning up the environment, and trying to save Planet Earth.

Recycle.

Support zoos, local nature centers, science centers, and other educational organizations that are working to protect wildlife and teach others about endangered animals.

Help others to understand that one of the biggest problems we face in the future is overpopulation of the human race. Two hundred years ago, there were less than one billion people on earth. Today, there are almost five billion people on earth competing for food, space, and limited resources. If the human population of the world continues to grow at its present rate, many species of plants and animals will disappear as more and more precious resources are depleted. Now is the time to do something to save Planet Earth!

Organizations that are making a big difference:

World Wildlife Fund
1250 24th Street, N.W.
Washington, D.C. 20037

National Wildlife Federation
1412 16th St., N.W
Washington, D.C. 20036

The Nature Conservancy
1815 N. Lynn Street
Arlington, Virginia 22209

National Audubon Society
950 Third Ave.
New York, New York 10022

There are many others on the state and local level. Do your part. Get involved!